"9 Key Website Optimization & SEO Strategies to Guarantee Website Conversion Success"

Turn your Website
Into a
Never Ending
Supply
Of New Leads, Sales & Inquiries

(For the Non Techie Person)

Warren Kannuck

PUBLISHED BY:
Warren Kannuck
Copyright © 2013

ISBN-13: 978-1500300098
ISBN-10: 1500300098

Are you sick of never getting any REAL Results From Your Website?

(And you just can't understand why!)

By the time you've finished reading through this book, you'll understand the reasons:

- Why you're website is not converting people into buyers, or inquiriers,
- Why your website isn't ranking in Google searches
- Why you're getting no results from your Adwords campaigns,
- Why people are leaving as fast as they arrive,
- Why you're not getting any calls or inquiries, AND
- Why your website is probably damaging your business or brand

AND you will also learn what it takes to FIX these problems once and for all.

What is it about a website that seems so appealing?

Everyone says you need one, and it seems as if there are literally hundreds of different ways you can get one. Some Web Developers charge thousands of dollars or pounds for a quality website, and then on the other hand there is practically every man and his dog trying to sell you their website creation expertise for pennies (or not much more).

So what is the truth? Do we need to spend hundreds or thousands on building ourselves a decent website? Can we create a website ourselves, or can we rely on the cheap options that are so readily bandied about?

But I guess one of the biggest questions you need to ask yourself is; "What are my expectations of this website?" and "What do I want it to do for me or my business?"

Before we get into the ins and outs of what actually makes a website work, you need to first understand the difference between a cheap website and a not so cheap website. Is it worth the investment spending all that money on a website from a high priced web developer when I could get my brother's girlfriends kid brother to build one for next to nothing? I mean at the end of the day, does it really make a difference?

The answer is a yes and no. (Not exactly what you expected right?) Well there are a lot of different dynamics that need to be taken into consideration when answering that question.

Without baffling you with a lot of techno speak, I'll do my best to answer this in easy to understand terminology.

There are a number of programming languages that are used when it comes to building websites. Unless you've done a degree in computer science, web development, or you've spent thousands of hours learning the ropes the hard way, then chances are you may know a little, but not much-am I right?

Perhaps you've heard of the acronyms; HTML, CSS, PHP? These are just a few of the many programming and scripting languages that are involved in the development of websites, and since the whole purpose of this book is to keep things simple, I won't go into the specific details of what they all are, or which ones might be the best.

When it comes to having a website built, one of the most important questions to ask yourself is; "Will I be able to self-manage the site?" In most instances, I'm hoping the answer is a very big YES. Because if you can't, then you will be forever dipping your hand into your wallet for new updates, changes you want done, new content, etc., you name it.

A lot of web development companies still develop websites and make it nearly impossible for the site owner to do anything on their site without first engaging them to do the work required.

As already mentioned this can get really expensive when you make a lot of changes or like to keep your site fresh and up to date.

Whereas on the other hand, there are companies that will build a great website for you on what is known as a CMS system or a 'Content Management System'.

This is the most practical form of website platform as it enables you to upload new content yourself, upload images, tweak the copy a little here, tweak it a little there and whilst many of these don't permit you to control the whole look and feel of the site, many do, and so if you are inclined to be a little more technically adventurous, you can adjust or even completely change or control the look and the feel and the layout of things on the site.

So in answer to the question of whether you need to spend a lot of money having your site developed, basically no you don't. As long as the person/company building your website fully understands the requirements of what it takes to make a site successful, and follows the guidelines outlined in this book and builds it on a platform that is both Search Engine friendly and allows you the ability to update it yourself as and when needed, then your site shouldn't need to cost a lot at all.

The exception to this rule is when you have specific requirements for your site that need 'custom coding' by a software expert, but for a standard site, that involves planning, designing, and construction from the ground up this shouldn't need to cost more than a few hundred dollars up to two or three thousand dollars. This indication is really only a guide and should be considered in light of the site itself and what your specific needs and requirements are. Also for on-going dedicated support and even copyrighting services, it can be worth it to pay more.

Consideration Point One

Always insist on an easy to use Content Management System when you are having a website created or built.

If you are adventurous and decide to go it alone then perhaps take a look at Wordpress, which is one of the most popular web building platforms. It's what we call 'Open Source' and is usually a free (or low priced) download.

Open Source is basically computer software where the Source Code of a particular program is made available (to anyone) with the rights for developers to makes changes, improvements, or even customize the Source Code. This is usually achieved through input from the public and other software developers and hence Open Source software often goes through an ever-evolving process from when it was first developed. The end user of the 'Open Source' Software (or their appointed web developer) effectively has control and responsibility for the Source Code.

Open Source software in relation to website development has a lot of detractors as well as a lot of advocates. At the end of the day, it's your choice as to which option you chose, however if you chose an Open Source platform, you will need to ensure all the updates that are needed are kept up to date yourself.

Wordpress and the variety of Plugins available provide a very sound CMS platform and it effectively provides no limits to the extent that you can customize the look, feel and layout of a website. Wordpress is the commonly used 'open source' web building platform in the world, although being Open Source, you will need to ensure that it (and its associated plugins) are constantly kept updated.

Otherwise there can be issues with the 'Search Engine' performance and security of the site over time and keeping the Software updated with the regular updates that Wordpress (and the plugin developers provide) will help your site remain up-to-date and secure. Also with Open Source software because of its very natures, you do run the ongoing and ever present threat of having your website hacked, which is the last thing you want happening if you become reliant on your site for sales, leads or inquiries.

Also consider some other alternatives of the Open Source options. Drupal, and Joomla are two other commonly used software platforms for building websites. They do usually require more understanding of the software and therefore the learning curve may be greater.

Beyond 'Open Source' platforms are the 'Proprietary Platforms'. These are Content Management Systems developed by various companies and organizations. Whilst these platforms may tie you into using a specific company to build and host your website, they also present some potential advantages over Open Source. For instance, there is often a great level of support. They often take care of all the various coding updates; ensuring the sites display effectively on new web browsers, ensuring the site is optimized for Search Engine Optimization purposes, they will usually back up the website on your behalf and they will usually be far more secure against hackers than 'Open Source'.

Another important factor here (as just alluded to above) is regular (ideally daily) backups of your website, so that if the worst did occur, at least you won't lose much time or opportunity. I have seen and met many business owners who never heeded this advice and suffered the consequences of a hacking incident. Be prepared, be warned and take out the relevant insurance by backing up.

OK So you now have your website platform organized. Now what? Are there a few key things to consider before you start having the website built?

Absolutely!

Consideration Point Two

How about a website plan?

Why do I need a website plan? Can't I just build the Home Page, and a few other pages, and then I'll be 'good to go'? Unfortunately no, an effective and successful website doesn't work like that.

Beware of the many web developers out there (particularly the really cheap ones) that tell you they will build you a 3 or 5 page website for $FREE (and all you have to do is pay them a monthly 'hosting fee') or up to $500. There's a very high likelihood that they won't mention a website plan to you and if you do happen to ask them about one, they may look at you blankly and say 'what do you mean?' This will indicate to you that they know very little if anything about how to make your website generate any genuine enquiries or sales, and so whilst you may actually end up with a site on the Internet, you've really just done your business a total disservice.

If leads, enquiries and ecommerce sales aren't part of your overall objective, then maybe this is fine for your business, but in my experience, when people arrive on your website, 80% of them make an instant judgment call on how 'professional' your business is (and consequently whether or not they will choose to engage YOUR business) simply by the look and layout of your site.

A lot of these types of developers are happy to throw up any old junk on the web using standard commonly available templates and then take your money in on-going monthly 'hosting' charges, but when it comes to service, back up, updates, etc. they are usually nowhere to be found. Sure many of these web developers may also be great at Graphic Design, or they may be great at developing code but many (probably most) of them give little or no consideration to your site being an effective "Sales and Marketing tool".

When you are really honest with yourself though, I'll bet that that's exactly what you want it to be; a Sales and Marketing tool to generate sales and leads, rather than some flashy, graphic mess that delivers no value to your visitor.

Honestly, you don't need some fancy schmancy looking site that brings in no enquiry. You don't need a quirky looking website with 'flash' that takes forever to load and brings in no sales. You want a website that floods you with enquiry, and leads, and sales –right?

Well let's take a look at the two things that will determine whether or not your website gets the results you are looking for.

Consideration Point Three

There are two key things that will determine whether you'll have a successful website or not and they are:

1) The number of visitors it receives, and
2) The conversion rate you have in turning these visitors into sales, enquiries or leads

That was easy now wasn't it? I guess that means we're at the end of the book?

Not quite, sorry.

There are a lot more key fundamentals than that to consider, which will determine your website's success or failure. You see most people have a website built, (or build it themselves) and think that's the finish line, then they think all they need to do is get as many visitors to the website as possible, which on the surface might seem like a great plan, but in reality that's not the correct approach to making a site successful.

Consider this question for a moment: Which of these two would you choose?

- A graphically brilliant, well designed site that had a real WOW factor visually, but yet no one ever enquired, or bought anything. OR
- A generally ugly site that had a never ending stream of people sending enquiries and sales to you

Most people that I know choose the second option.

Now ask yourself this: If I had 1000 visitors to my website per month, and yet 1000 people left without calling me, emailing me, or buying anything- would that represent a successful site to you?

I thought not.

When it comes to visitors arriving at your site, there are generally five main aspects that will determine whether your visitor stays and ultimately decides to do what you want them to do; which as we all know is to either call you, make an enquiry, or buy something from you.

So, you really need to get your conversion rate right first before you contemplate spending money in marketing to get as many visitors to the site as possible.

AND, with your Conversion rate; you need to be constantly and regularly testing, measuring and improving various elements on your site, so that you can determine which of these elements are most effective at getting people to 'do what you want them to do'.

Consideration Point Four

The Conversion Rate

1) The first thing to get right with your website

Think about how you respond when you first arrive at a website. Do you get impatient if it doesn't download in about 3 or 4 seconds, and you're onto the next website? A lot of studies have shown that if a site takes longer than 3 or 4 seconds to download then up to 40% of the visitors are likely to leave your site without even having seen the first page. (How much is that likely to impact on your desired goals for the site?)

With the massive uptake of smartphones in recent times, there can be as much as 30-40% of Internet searches being undertaken using these mobile devices.

The word on the street is that within a few more years mobile Internet search will overtake searches done from desktops and laptops. Also because the mobile Internet connections are still a little slower than standard broadband connections, and signal and capacity issues also play a major role in overall download speeds the expectation for a site to download on one of these mobile devices is a little less demanding. The rule of thumb is that a site should download on a mobile device within about 8-10 seconds

2) The second thing to get right

Assuming the site does download in the required time, what's the next thing you do? Normally you'll take a quick look around the page looking for some highly visible headline or bold statement that answers the question(s) you have or provides you with a statement that makes sense to you.

Typically when people go to a website, they have some questions sitting in the back of their heads that they want or need answers to, and again of your website doesn't provide enough of a benefit, or doesn't address the questions they have prominently on your Home page, then again many people will just think you don't offer what they are looking for and will leave.

Therefore the layout of your site needs to comply with the internationally accepted standard for modern website layout.

What is this standard for a layout?

Well typically you need your name and business logo in the top left hand corner of the site. Ideally you'll have a phone number or email address prominently displayed on the right hand top corner. The navigation or menu bar needs to be either along the top, or down the left (never on the right). There needs to be an easily located About Us, and Contact Us page, preferably in the navigation or menu bar, and finally there needs to be a footer area at the bottom of the page.

Your site also needs to have an 'Easy to use' feel. Layout is a very big part of this, as people expect a website to be intuitively laid out. They don't expect to have go in search for what they are looking for.

What say you want to include some 'flash' video, or images on your home page to create that moving effect? This can look pretty cool right? Well in short, the answer to this is a resounding 'Don't do it' The reasons behind this is that typically 'Flash' on a Home Page will significantly slow your load times, and hence if this results in a load time of around 7-8 seconds or more, then you can probably kiss goodbye to nearly half your visitors and you don't want that to happen do you?

The second reason is because 'Flash' and Apple mobile devices (Iphones, ipads, ipods) are not able to display 'flash' and hence with mobile becoming one of the fastest growing segments for internet search, currently representing as much as 30-40% of all internet searches these days, you may be missing out on around 10-20% of your visitors who might be using an ipad or iphone. By simply utilizing standard jpg images you can generally achieve a similar desired effect but with the hassles that can lose you up to half of your potential site visitors.

Finally, people like to use 'Flash' to try and create some quirky, funky modern look and feel. Please don't be fooled into doing this either. Any web developer trying to convince you to do this has no idea about getting results for your site. Chances are they will be a Graphic designer and nothing more, they won't know how to generate visitors to your site, or how to convert them into sales, enquiries, or leads.

Visitors don't go to your website to be challenged by some quirky creative home page that doesn't make any sense, or is difficult to navigate around. People these days are time poor, and the more roadblocks and obstacles you put in front of front of your website visitor the more likely you are to lose them altogether.

Take a good look at your competitors' websites. If they are all quirky and funky, then great their website visitors will be leaving them in droves and it presents a massive opportunity for you (to get it right). If on the other hand they look sophisticated, professional and modern, then they've got it right, and you should not contemplate stepping out of that norm either. (Or perhaps I should say, do so at your peril)

3) The Third thing to get right

If a stranger looking like a homeless person was to walk up to you in the middle of the street and showing you the keys offer to sell you a brand new luxury car that they said they had just won in a lottery and all you had to do was to go and get $5000 in cash to give to them and then the car was yours- Would you? Or would you tend to think this isn't right, there's something fishy going on here! Most people would run a mile. On other hand if that same offer was made to you by someone you know and trust, you might still think it a little odd, but chances are you might be more willing to take them up on their amazing offer.

The point we're making here is it all comes down to trust and credibility. We will generally only do business with people we like, people we know (and like) and people we trust. So how can you engender trust in a visitor to your website? They normally don't know you from a bar of soap, and sure you may have a pretty website that looks very professional, but how do they know you aren't just another 'take my money and run' type of business?

This is when establishing your business, or your website's credibility becomes vitally important. How can you achieve this?

Well there are a number of ways that you do this.

There is an interesting statistic that you need to be very mindful of and that is that approximately 75% to 80% of people visiting your website will make an instant judgment about your business based on their immediate perception of your website. If you present an easy to use, professional website, they will give you an initial tick in the back of their mind and will likely continue on looking for whatever it is they are looking for.

On the other hand if you present a very amateurish, unprofessional looking site that is difficult to navigate or isn't easy to find what you're looking for, then there is every likelihood you will lose them off the site altogether. Hence the first part of Trust and credibility is all about first impressions.

To create the inbuilt elements of trust on a website, you (often) need to go into a lot of detail about the business. No longer is a simple paragraph or two about what you're trying to do in business any good. We're talking here about the "About Us" page. This page would probably be the most important page of your whole website (after the Home page). On the 'About Us' page you need to go into a great deal of detail as to how your business started, what its history is, what your point of difference is, and who runs the business.

Not only should it include this type of information, but it can even pay to go so far as to include some photos of the key personnel involved in the business and a brief bio about each of these people. The reason behind this is because people like to do business with other people and not a website.

They like to know (or at least have the opportunity to relate and perhaps even empathize with) the people that are at the heart of this website. If you can win them over through a really effective 'About Us' page, then you've already won half the battle, so don't scrimp on content when creating this page. It will make all the difference to your conversion rates.

Another element that can be fundamentally important here is having your 'Contact Us' page include a physical address and landline phone number. Why is that important? Many people like to do business with someone that they feel has a real physical presence somewhere.

Any website that hides behind a P.O Box number and/or a mobile number loses credibility, as it reeks of 'Home business' or worse perhaps even 'scammer'. If you are Home based business and this is obvious from your type of website, then do consider including your physical address, or perhaps even look at renting a virtual serviced office for the purpose of having an actual physical location on your website.

Does your website offer the visitor or prospective client some form of Solid Guarantee. For example, if you're selling products on your site, do you offer a '100% Money Back guarantee'? Or if you're promoting and selling some type of service, do you offer a "Satisfaction Guarantee- If you don't feel we delivered exactly on our Service promise, we will refund you 110% of your purchase price" These type of guarantees give people confidence to buy from you.

Are you starting to see now how having a legitimate physical address, a decent money back or satisfaction guarantee and valid substantial information about who they are dealing with in your 'About Us' page is starting to build a reasonable amount of trust in your business already?

So what else is important to include on your website that will add to your trust and credibility?

How about some 'preselling page(s)'?

Preselling pages are pages of information about your products or services generally, or they may even be about some related topic where you AREN'T trying to sell the visitor anything. You are purely informing them about a subject matter that will more than likely inspire them take a closer look at what products and services you do offer. Preselling pages can be decent articles, even videos that provide an educational component to the visitor. Feel free to use these widely. They do have the added advantage that if they are separate pages on your site (with their own unique URL) then they can even bring you added traffic (more visitors) to your website.

Now that the visitor is pretty warmed up about who you are, what you're about, and that you a reputable type of business online, the next step should be the one that takes them to the edge of their seat, and remove any doubts they may have had about buying from you, and that is through the use of Testimonials, and Case Studies. Testimonials and Case Studies are quite different beasts, and whilst there are some people out there that completely dispute the effects of testimonials, a Case Study or two can be less disputable.

Testimonials definitely have their place and using two or three can help but in reality most people will disregard them if you only have a handful of testimonials. After all you might have 96 disgruntled and unhappy customers and 4 highly ecstatic ones, and obviously it's the 4 that you will publish on your website. So whatever you don't treat your visitor as if they are stupid.

Don't create artificial testimonials and don't put up brief one liner testimonials that end in 'signed- A Happy Customer' – nothing loses credibility faster than a generic testimonial like that. If you're going to use testimonials (and I strongly suggest that you do) try and use at least half a dozen, and try and get them to be two or three sentence testimonials (ie a small paragraph) and try and get the testimonial giver to allow you to use their full name, location and possibly even a photo (if they'll supply it). Then, when you publish them to your website you'll have half a dozen (perhaps more) very powerful statements from contented happy customers that look truthful because they have full names, locations and perhaps even a photo next to them.

A case study has even more power than a testimonial. A case study often requires a bit of research before writing it, but with the time spent on creating the case study it should return you well with enhanced trust and credibility. A case study is like a story.

Begin your case study with the 'Before' situation for the client, highlighting their problem or their issue, and the solution or the fix that you recommended, and then the 'After' which was after their issue or problem was rectified or fixed through implementing your recommended solution. To top the case study off, add the testimonial that you received from this client as a footnote.

Used well, Case Studies and testimonials have awesome power and prove to prospective clients that you are a reputable business to deal with and are capable of providing solutions to their problems or issues.

There are a number of other elements that should be added to the site to further enhance your credibility. Such as:

- Various Policies; 'Privacy Policy', (so people understand your policy about keeping their information private and secure, and that you don't go and re-sell this to some other third party) Your 'Terms of Trade' (so people understand the terms under which they buy from you. This may often cover things like credit accounts, charge backs, refunds, returns policies, etc.)
- Has your business received 'Awards' or recognition for some achievement? Has it been the recipient of various 'Certifications', or 'Qualifications'?
- Does your business support any local initiatives, or does it sponsor any charities or other Community based groups? This is all worth promoting if it does, especially if much of your business is likely to come from the local community.
- Is your business associated with, or does it represent some well-known brand names? If you're able to, or allowed to you should utilize the advantage and credibility you can acquire from presenting these brand images on your website. Do you have any affiliations or partnerships with any well-known respected Organisations that you can also use some borrowed credibility from?
- Finally, have there been any promotional features that were published in the media about your business? If so, use these to their maximum, or if not, and you have some noteworthy news to report, then perhaps make contact with media organisations and see if they

might be interested in promoting your news story.

4) The fourth thing to get right with your website

The final thing you need to get right for your website is all about optimizing it to maximize your conversions.

What can you do to improve conversion rates for your site? It's not a difficult concept, but you need to have very clearly planned and created pathways for people to follow. What this means is that each page of your website needs strongly structured and carefully and powerfully worded 'headlines'. The content on each of these pages needs to be powerfully worded especially if it is sales focused.

Each of these content pages needs to have some 'pre planned' connection to other pages on your site and on each of these pages, there needs to be a strong "Call to Action". Basically all your website's pages need to direct the visitor to your 'eventual desired result' page, which is likely to be the enquiry page, the sales page, or the subscription page.

Your conversion rates will increase significantly if you have this pathway very clearly structured beforehand and you know exactly what the objective and purpose of your site is and you build the whole website accordingly.

Take a look around at a lot of websites and you'll discover that there are a very high percentage of sites that have NO 'Calls to Action' at all. The site owner assumes the visitor will know where to go to next. Much like sales, where many sales are lost simply because a salesperson never ASKS for the sale, a website is no different. You need to tell the visitor where to go next, or at least give them a couple of clickable options so they have a choice (but you still need to tell them to click on them and where it will take them to)

5) The fifth thing to get right with your website.

These days, everyone has gone 'mobile'. Your website needs to have an effective means of displaying its content on a mobile device. Whether it be an iphone, an android, an ipad, or a tablet. There availability of screen sizes these days seems endless. So, how do websites display on mobile devices?

The answer for many is poorly. The poor visitor has to pinch and zoom in to view the content, or they have to scroll backwards and forwards to read it. Many just get too frustrated and leave, only to visit your competitor who does have a site that displays effectively.

Also, the Google Search Results are weighted in favor of websites that will display more effectively on mobile devices. So if, you don't have a 'mobile optimized site', you are adversely affecting your chances of showing up in Google Searches.

There are generally two ways a website can be displayed on your device.

- As a dedicated separate mobile website.

  These versions are the least favored (in my opinion) as they present the user with a 'cut down' version of the primary website. You may have seen these yourself, where they present you with small tabs, that generally have the main Navigation on them, ie Home, About us, Services, Contact Us, etc.

The detail on these tabs when you click on them is often insufficient for the visitor to make decisions and so again they often leave your site. Another issue with these types of mobile site, is they mean you now have a secondary website to manage and maintain. (I don't know about you, but most business owners I know struggle to maintain one website, let alone two).

You'll often recognize these types of sites by the url; They may have
http://m.businessname at their start.

Another way is that at the end of their website, they may have the option of converting between a 'desktop version' and a 'mobile version'.

Whilst this type of mobile option is the least preferred, it is still better to have something rather than nothing.

- Having 'Responsive Design' Software incorprated into your primary website

This is the preferred mobile display method. Because the software is structured into your primary site, you only have a single website to manage and maintain.

The way the site displays on a mobile device is reformatted by the software, so that ALL the website's content is displays on the device. Eerything is structurally lined up in a 'vertical only' scrolling format. The text is easy to read with no pinching or zooming required, and the software also 're-orients' the display of the site based on the size of screen viewing it.

You need to make it easy for your visitors to view and interact with your website, and present a few obstacles as possible. Giving them a great mobile experience is one of those key requirements.

6) Is there anything else I can do on an on-going basis to improve my website's conversion rates?

Yes there are but this comes down to the type of site you have and the available functionalities you have on your site. If you have the capability to do 'Split Testing' on your website, then you are blessed with a tool that can help you to potentially double your conversion rates over the course of the next year or two.

If you happen to have decided on the Wordpress.org platform, (where you self-host your own website using the downloadable Wordpress Content management System) then there are 'third party' Split Testing plugins you can download and incorporate into your site to enable you to run Split Tests.

Split testing is where you can take a particular page of your website, and ideally replicate it and then change one particular component of the page, perhaps a headline, or an image, or a Call to action. The main thing with Split testing is that you can effectively measure two variants of the same page over a period of time and then run with the version that works best.

Consideration Point Five

Getting your website ranked in Google- so you can get the Visitors (traffic)

This is the part where we now address your visitors to the site. Assuming you've taken care of the conversion rate, you've optimized and set this up so that your 'leaky bucket' syndrome is no longer hemorrhaging visitors through the massive holes you had in the bucket, and now there are a fair number of enquiries and leads coming in. As a rule of thumb, a good conversion rate should be between 3-5% based on International statistics.

Realistically this section though could probably cover a book the size of the old Encyclopedia Britannica, but as we don't have the space or time to provide that much detail here, we will try and keep it succinct, brief and to the point.

Getting visitors to your website is now your main focus.

Firstly, you need to understand about keywords, and which keywords are the main focus for your site. Having a sound understanding of keywords will help you to create appropriate 'traffic generating' content for your site.

Why is this important?

Not many people know it, but only about 20% of your visitors will arrive on your Home page, the balance will probably arrive through other pages on your site and interestingly enough only about 50% of your traffic comes from Search Engine results pages. That tells you that a lot of the external marketing, word of mouth, people that know you or your brand will find your website directly.

If you want to understand which keywords are the most searched for terms for your business, head off to the Google Keyword Tool. (The keyword tool within Google has changed over the years. Keyword research tools using Google is now under the Adwords umbrella- Use the Google tutorials and guides to get the best value from this). This Google free service will provide you with literally hundreds or thousands of keyword terms you never even contemplated for your business and it will supply you with an approximation as to how many people are searching for the phrase per month. There are alternative third party tools (that cost money to purchase) that will automate keyword research for you (such as Market Samurai)

When you do a keyword search in Google, be careful to select the correct search option. The most reliable one is usually 'phrase match, or 'exact match' rather than broad match. The broad match option is usually that too broad. If you put a couple of words into a phrase, then a broad match will search the web for any of those words in any order, and bring up a lot of irrelevant results, whereas phrase and exact are much more targeted.

Consideration Point Six

So why are Keywords important for my website?

Keywords are uniquely important because that's what people use to search for things on the web. You know how you open up a Google Search page, you type in what you're looking for, and then Google comes back with a whole bunch of results that seemingly goes on forever page after page? That's why keyword phrases are important, because Google needs to understand and be aware of what your website is all about if you want to have any hope of ranking on the first couple of search result pages. (If you're on page 3 or beyond, then you won't ever see any notable traffic at all as all traffic usually comes from page one, and to a lesser extent occasionally from page two)

Meta Data, Meta Content or Meta tags are also really important to understand. The Meta Title & the Meta Description are the two components that a website admin enters for each of the site's pages. It is this data that Google picks up and displays on its Search Results pages.

See below for an example of a search result as displayed for the key phrase 'Website Builder'. (This is a fictitious search result- but is highlighted to show you the importance of Meta content)

This result usually shows up with another 9 examples, (10 per page) and is often referred to as the Organic Search results.

<u>WEBSITE BUILDER</u> by SuchaSuch Co. Create a Website Easily!

www.**suchasuch**.com/Share

WEBSITE BUILDER by SuchaSuch Co is a handy tool to create a website in minutes. You will easily make a website and put it online. Absolutely no skills required.

The first line *"**Website Builder** by SuchaSuch Co. Create a Website Easily!"* is your Meta Title.

And the sentence *"**Website builder** by SuchaSuch Co is a handy tool to create a website in minutes. You will easily make a website and put it online. Absolutely no skills required."* is your Meta Description.

If the Meta Description is missing then Google will grab the first 160 characters it can find on your website. Usually this is the first few words on your site. That's NOT good, especially if you have advertising at the top of your page or you've wasted this valuable virtual real estate with a phrase like "Welcome to our web site" at the top of your page – How much information does that tell your potential visitor (or Google for that matter) – So please, don't EVER use the phrase 'Welcome to my/our website' as this will do you absolutely no favours when it comes to ranking your site anywhere - ever!

Consideration Point Seven

OK, so how do I make my site readable by Google so I get ranked?

That is the lifelong question people keep asking. In fact this whole subject has an industry all of its own. Have you ever heard the term "Search Engine Optimization" or "SEO" for short?

This is the supposed study of what it takes to get websites ranked for keyword terms and there are two parts to SEO: Off Page and On Page. The fundamental differences are that 'On Page' is to do with everything you can control about your website, and 'Off Page' is to do with everything outside of your website. The whole SEO Optimization subject is filled with lots of varying opinions as to what is required for ranking with Google, and to top it all off Google keeps changing the rules and moving the goalposts. With more than 200 algorithms that they use to determine how relevant a website page is, it can become quite a challenge to get things right, especially as Google keeps updating its requirements.

Assuming Google's robots have found and indexed your website and its pages, then the ranking process can begin and the most important thing you should focus on in your attempt to be ranked for specific keywords is your 'On Page' SEO aspects.

By the way, beware of any organization offering SEO services to you where they promise or guarantee number one status on Page one. You need to be aware that no one can promise number one on page one. Its possible SEO techniques can get you there, but no-one can promise or guarantee it. So if you encounter anyone making such promises-run a mile!

There was a recent private survey undertaken which showed up some very interesting results concerning what it apparently takes to rank in the first five results for a search phrase. The results tend to support a lot about what we already know when it comes to ranking a page for a particular search phrase.

The survey involved 100 random keyword search phrases that consisted of a mix of 2 word phrases up to 6 word phrases. The top five ranking sites for each of these keyword phrases were then analyzed for similarities and consistencies. The searches were undertaken using the Firefox browser, and no one was logged into any Google products or account at the time.

The results covered a number of different data elements, and whilst not claiming to be perfect it does provide a really useful indicator to the novice as to what is required of their site and their pages to hopefully have a chance to rank well in search engine results pages.

Consideration Point Eight

In a nutshell the key determinants picked up from the survey that seemed to make a difference were:

Re 'On Page' Optimization

- The word count on a webpage should be around 900 words on average. At the end of the day, we all know Google loves great content, and preferably fresh and new content. Another thing to pay attention to here is that 900 words can be quite a lot of content to wade through, so a great technique to incorporate here to make it easy for everyone to read your content is to break up much of the content into paragraphs with relevant catchy headlines. Because some people love long copy and some people love short copy, you need to appeal to both. Breaking the copy into sections with headlines makes long copy easy to read, and also still keeps it interesting for the short copy reader.

- In the Meta Title tag, most of the sites that ranked highly used the exact keyword phrase in the Meta Title tag. The Meta Title is one of the most important components for each web page as it tells Google principally what your page is about. Traditionally it is recommended that a Meta Title include a couple of main keyword phrases and perhaps the business name or brand. Ideally the Meta Title tag should be kept to around 60 characters at an optimum.

- The Meta Description is also a very important element for Google (and the human reader). The Meta Description should be different for every page of the site, and it should consist of a strong powerful value proposition for the page of approximately 160 characters. It should contain the main key phrase but also it is really important that it reads easily but with a compelling message, after all, it will be the human visitor that clicks on the Google search result only if it provides them with an interesting reason to want to click.

- The keyword density (the frequency, or how often a keyword phrase shows up in the body content of the page) was relatively lower than expected. The keyword density for the key phrases analysed was only around 0.5 of 1%. Meaning for every 1000 words on content the key phrase would only be mentioned about 5 times at most, however it did reveal that the use of the 'exact key phrase' only once seemed to be enough.

- Sub-Headings seemed to be relatively important as the average of the high ranking pages had 6 subheadings and these also included keywords where relevant if it made sense.

- Incorporating images within the content seemed to help with rankings

The most important thing that came out of the study from an 'On Page' point of view is that the content should be written to read as naturally as possible and any over optimization should be left out altogether.

Re 'Off Page' Optimization

- Ranking for Internal web pages seemed to be higher than actual home pages. This may be because Home Pages are usually over-optimized for a 'harder to rank for' broad key phrase whereas internal pages can often rank better for more specific better targeted key phrases.

- The result for back linking effectiveness still showed that back links are relevant and important. The Google number 1 ranking site for the key phrase still had on average five times more back links than the site ranked at position 5

- Social media and social interactions seem to also play a part in the rankings. An observation of the results of the study highlighted that sites ranked highly had over twice as many Tweets, around 10 times the Facebook likes, and double the Facebook shares as their lower ranking competing sites.

The most important lesson learned in the study for Off Page Optimization is that back links, whereby another site is linking back to your site or pages (and having as many back links as possible) is still one of the most important aspects of ranking websites as far as Google seems to be concerned.

So there you have it.

Consideration Point Nine

The summary of what you should now know.

- Structure

You now should have everything you need to know to help select the right platform to build your website and how to structure your website effectively so that you can update content yourself and have a site that is easy to use and follows the international layout conventions

- Content

You also should have everything you need to know to enable you to enrich your site with the right amount of key phrase focused content along with the right amount of catchy headlines, and sub headings, all whilst keeping an eye on the keyword density so as not to over optimize your content.

- Meta Content

You now know how important it is to get your Meta Title and Meta Description right by including some relevant targeted (well searched for) key phrases that will appeal to Google's robots as well as the human reader.

- Backlinks

You now know that having a large number of back links is important to your Google rankings. Spend some time learning how to generate some backlinks. Comment on blogs, contribute to the Social chats, write a few articles, submit a press release occasionally, and publish a YouTube video. The ways to generate back links are endless.

- Social Media

You now know that you need to get yourself setup with a Facebook page for your business to compliment your website. Setup a Twitter profile as well. Also look at LinkedIn. Regularly participate in the chats online on these Social platforms and over time it will pay dividends in terms of visitors to your website

- Structured Conversion Pathway

You now know how important it is to have a planned and organized pathway for your visitors to navigate through as well as having strong and convincing Headlines and Calls to Action

- Loading Times

You now know how important load times are for your website so you don't lose half your potential visitors before they even land on your site. Much of the time taken for a page to download will be determined by the software platform you chose to build your site on as well as your images and whether or not these are compressed and optimized for displaying readily on your website

- Trust & Credibility

You now know how important it is to engender trust in your visitors as early as possible because you now know that if your visitors don't trust you or you have no credibility with them, they won't engage with you, or call you or contact you and your conversion rates will be very low.

Conclusion

I do hope you have enjoyed reading this book, and that you have found the information in it enlightening. There is a lot to consider when it comes to creating a website and the more time and effort you put into planning it strategically and logically the more effective it will be for you. Also don't scrimp on content and especially don't get your content written by someone who does a cheap job. It will cost you in the long run.

Think of your website much like you would taking on a new sales person assuming you were the boss. Would you just provide them with some cheap information that they need to learn, ask them to learn it all, and then send them on their merry way telling them 'Please bring me lots of leads, and sales over the next 12 months' as they departed?

Of course you wouldn't.

More than likely you would train them well ensuring they had all the right 'up to date' knowledge and access to all the content they needed. You would show them how to sell by providing them with a structured pathway to making the sale, and then you would ensure they stayed up to date and no doubt you'd hand hold them over the next 12 months constantly working with them to improve and be more successful at selling and providing them whatever they needed to help them bring in the sales.

A website is no different. It needs your on-going attention to thrive, improve and stay up to date too. So what sort of boss are you?

I hope you loved this book and that it provided you with lots of insights to improve your website. If you could kindly please take a moment to provide me with a review on Amazon, I'd really appreciate it.

I wish you well in your future endeavours.

If you enjoyed this book, I would love it if would give me your honest review on Amazon

You can leave your review by searching on the Amazon search bar, the title of this book:

"9 Key Website Optimization & SEO Strategies to Guarantee Website Conversion Success"

Check out these other Kindle eBooks by Warren Kannuck

How to Overcome Every Sales Objection

Suggestions and guidance on how to maximize your sales by overcoming the variety of objections you might experience.

Starting a New Business on a Shoestring

How to get started in business on a bare-bones budget as well as a lot of different business ideas as suggestions.

The Secrets to Becoming a Successful Telemarketer

Everything you need to know to be a successful telemarketer (or improve your cold calling skills)

www.ingramcontent.com/pod-product-compliance
Lightning Source LLC
Chambersburg PA
CBHW051225170526
45166CB00005B/2045